Nine stories of healing and death

Tell 'em
Charlie
Sent 'ya

by
BRENDA HARTMAN

First Steps Publishing

Tell 'em Charlie Sent 'ya

© 2011 by Brenda Hartman.

First Printing CreateSpace

This book does not attempt to diagnose or treat cancer or any other illness. The information presented is not intended to replace the advice of health-care professionals. The stories described are real, but names and certain details have been changed to protect identities.

Print ISBN #978-0-9882103-1-8
eBook ISBN #978-0-9882103-0-1

Editor: Karen Carpenter
Cover design by Suzanne Fyhrie Parrott
Formatted and published by First Steps Publishing

Printed in the United States of America

In Honor of my Mother Gerry,
Gramma Chooch,
Ione
and all those who have gone before me.

ACKNOWLEGDEMENTS

There are many people I would like to thank who have helped me with this book. First and foremost, I offer gratitude to all the individuals who allowed me to walk with them to their physical death. I also thank all the thousands of other cancer patients I have met and worked with along the way. My children, Maria and Robbie, have been guides and an honor to know. Gratitude for all of my family and friends who have stayed next to me through all of my living. Special thanks to my editor, Karen Carpenter, who stood next to me, encouraging me to continue writing and helping me to ensure these stories conveyed their deepest meaning. And to my publisher, Suzanne Fyhrie Parrott, a deep and heartfelt thank you for her amazing guidance, support, patience and belief in publishing this book.

CONTENTS

INTRODUCTION

I am not supposed to be alive right now. In 1988, my diagnosis was stage four ovarian cancer. According to statistics at that time, I had a five percent chance of living 24 months, and no one lived beyond 24 months.

I was a graduate student at the U of M and I was diagnosed between classes. I was working on two PhD's. I went to have an outpatient procedure, because they thought I had endometriosis. It turns out that I had stage four ovarian cancer! They did not expect me to live. I was hospitalized for chemotherapy treatments, had multiple surgeries and two near-death experiences. I had a "spontaneous remission," or I was a "medical mystery," or "a miracle occurred" (many phrases have been used to describe what happened) and I lived. My oncologist told me that I am alive because of what I did, since what they did to me should have killed me.

For over 20 years I have pondered why I lived. I spent a great amount of time exploring, researching and reading about other cultural and religious beliefs to expand my personal understanding of life and death. This was important to me since the religious and cultural beliefs I had grown up with had not helped me face my own death or understand how I could still be alive. My life path has brought me to many places I never imagined. I shredded two dissertations and started a third which would explore the allopathic and indigenous forms of healing and how they can work together. Then I shredded that dissertation.

Today I am a psychotherapist (MSW, LICSW) in private practice with a specialization in oncology. Working with cancer patients, their families and support teams is a gift to me. We talk honestly about the physical, emotional and spiritual experience of living with a life-threatening disease. I walk next to cancer patients when they are in treatment, between treatments, in remission, and, in many cases, as they walk to their death. These patients have honored me by sharing their leaving processes as described in this book. They have taught me a great deal about life and death. I want to share some of their stories so others may learn from them, too. In the past, I shared these stories with individuals walking to their death, and they told me the stories were helpful to them. I met all of the cancer patients in these stories when they came to me seeking therapy after they had been diagnosed with cancer and were in treatment. None of them were facing their death directly when we met, but through the course of our work together, death became imminent. It is from that point of view that these stories were written.

Death can be difficult to discuss. We all have an emotional response to death. The dominant upper Midwestern culture often creates a resistance to an open conversation regarding death, seemingly rising from a belief that anyone talking about death is asking to die. When I was in treatment, I was so sick and in so much pain I wanted to die; but I did not die, even when I wanted to.

There is also the belief that if we talk about dying we are giving up hope. I disagree. When someone is diagnosed with cancer I believe we are all thinking about death; his, hers, mine, yours, those who have died.... It requires a lot of energy to have thoughts about death, and even more to keep them hidden as if there is something wrong with them. When I meet people, death is one of our first discussion topics.

The English language does not have many words to describe death, the feelings around death, or the spiritual changes that many times take place. Because of this, I have created certain terms and phrases to help us communicate about these topics.

People come to me wanting to know how I healed. I know everything in my life lead up to it. It was much more complicated than doing the one right thing. I did many things. One of the most important things I did was to prepare for my death. I did this twice - when I was first diagnosed, and again when I was actively dying, right before my spontaneous remission. I found that by preparing for my death, I could focus all of my energy on living. When thoughts and fears about my death came up, I had a way to respond and could then return my focus to living.

I am not interested in anyone believing what I believe. My intention in stating my beliefs is to provide a still point for others to push against and discover what they believe and why. I believe we all have separate healing paths and our complete healing occurs when we die physically to this earth. So I suggest, when asking for healing, ask only for a 95% healing so one can stay in the physical world.

Since my second near-death experience, I think/see mentally in pictures. It is as though the door between this world and the other world (where we go when we die) was blown off and I can no longer close the door. Images come through to me. I have used these images or pictures to help me describe concepts when I am meeting with cancer patients. One image of life and death is that we are all walking on the road of life. We each have a personal fork on the road which leads off the main road and takes us to our physical death. To consciously live and consciously die we become aware of, and look for, our personal fork in the road.

When a cancer patient is first diagnosed, for many people it is their first sense of their own death. Prior to that experience, we all walk around knowing about death, saying, "it happens to all of us," and "you can't get out of here alive," but we don't really have a sense of what that might mean. When cancer patients are with me, we discuss ways to prepare for death/healing while actively living. I refer to this as "coming even with life and death." One of my first homework assignments for my patients is to create a list of things they want to complete before they die. We discuss wills, funeral plans, obituaries, dispersal of physical property, letters to be written, and all the other details of life that an individual may want to complete. This list is different for each person. Following that, we move on to what needs to occur to say goodbye to the people we love. This brings a person into consciously living each moment they have with their loved ones. On multiple occasions, I have witnessed the relief of stress upon completion of this list. Patients focus on living each moment and they live moments / days / weeks / months / years longer than was ever predicted by the medical statistics. I call this game "stump the docs." While scratching their heads, the docs respond with "I don't know why you are doing as well as you are, but we are pleased about it."

I imagine us having two parts-the physical body, which I refer to as a "vessel," and our spirit or soul - that part which leaves the physical body when we say that a person has died. I have witnessed individuals consciously walking to their physical death on their fork in the road and many times they have awareness from both parts of themselves, their physical body / mind and spirit / soul on the other side. Often when people are in both places at once, they are able to speak from both places. Many times I have heard people use the term "we" when they are speaking from their spirit/soul perspective. I understand the use of "we" to refer to words coming from the individual's soul in connection with other souls: Great Spirit, God, Jesus, Allah, Waken Tankan, the One who Goes by a Thousand Names and the One who is Nameless. This is difficult to explain in English words. In all cases, when I have heard individuals using the word "we" in this way, there was something which clarified their intention to be speaking from the point of view of a collective, something greater than the individual's personal understanding or knowing.

Many individuals in an active dying state have shared with me a variety of thoughts, including: they can feel/tell that "my door" to the other side is open, that they trust me to guide them to the other side; they know I will walk over with them so they will not be alone, etc. The first time I was told this I was surprised and confused. I wondered what they saw and felt when they were with me. I have been told this many times now, so I am no longer surprised and find comfort in trusting that my soul and the soul of the individual telling me this are working together, beyond my conscious understanding.

What follows are stories from some of the people I walked with as they approached their death. These stories are from my point of view. I am confident that any other person witnessing these events would describe them differently. We all take in different information from any experience we share. Any parent or child on a family vacation will return home remembering different aspects of the time spent together. The events/stories within are the same. There are no right or wrong descriptions, just mine. May they be helpful to you.

CHARLIE

I met Charlie when he had been through several phases of cancer treatment and had more to go. We talked about conscious living and conscious dying. We explored ways to think about his treatment as healing and moving forward, living each day we are alive and dying all at once.

I shared my belief that life is a process of healing, and that the ultimate healing occurs when we die to the physical world. I see life as a road on which we all have our own individual path. For each of us, there is a fork in the road which leads to our final healing, i.e., death to the physical world.

Charlie was a young man of 35 years. He was married and had a three-year old son. His family was actively involved in his support. There was a time when Charlie was no longer able to come into my office, so I went to his home. We talked about the fork in the road.

One day when I arrived at his house, his mother answered the door and told me she was sorry no one had called to tell me that Charlie had been in a coma for the previous two days. I asked her if I could say goodbye to Charlie.

Charlie was in a hospital bed, looking very thin and breathing slowly. I sat in a chair next to Charlie to say goodbye. To this day, I do not know if I spoke out loud or just in my head. But Charlie turned his head toward me, opened his eyes and said he needed some water! He got out of bed and began walking to the kitchen.

I looked down the hallway at his mother as I followed behind Charlie, my arms out to catch him if he fell. His mother raised her hands and mouthed "What did you do?" I mouthed back "I didn't do anything!"

We got water for Charlie and propped him up in a chair with pillows. After working to drink some water through a straw, Charlie turned to his mother and asked her to leave. By this time, Charlie's mother knew I would share what was about to transpire when Charlie and I were done talking.

Once she left, Charlie turned to me and said "I have become twins and soon I will become one again." Not knowing what he meant or what I should say, I asked the classic therapist question, "Could you say a little more about that?" Charlie went on to recall our conversations regarding the fork in the road, conscious living and conscious dying. He knew he had become twins, one twin on each road. He explained that if he becomes one with the twin here in the physical world, he will have a spontaneous remission of his cancer and be able to go outside to throw the ball to his son, instead of laying in bed listening to him play outside.

Charlie also explained that if he became one with the other twin, "We know it will be for the greater good. And we know that everyone will be fine - my wife, my son, my family, everyone." At this point I asked Charlie if he was speaking to me from the other side. He turned, looked at me, and with a smile he spoke from the twin on the other side, saying "Yes we are."

He told me how each twin knew that be-coming one with either would be for "the greater good." I asked him if I could speak to others about our conversation. With a big smile he responded, "Why do you think we have been waiting for you? You have many people to share this with." I asked him exactly what he wanted me to say to others. With laughter he said "Tell 'em Charlie sent ya!"

I then asked Charlie if there was anything he needed. Charlie informed me he did not want to stay at the house, because he did not want his son to grow up in the house where he died. I said I would tell his family so they could make arrangements to get him to the hospital. I said goodbye and thanked Charlie for being in my life.

When I returned to the living room, Charlie's wife was coming in the door. Charlie's mother had called to let her know that Charlie was awake and talking with me. I let them both know that Charlie had asked to be moved to the hospital to die. As I left their house, they went to speak with Charlie and make arrangements.

Charlie's wife called me from the hospital the next day. She informed me that they had been able to transport Charlie to the hospital and were all there now. She also said that they had the chance to speak with Charlie before he returned to a comatose state. Now, however, he had just awakened and called my name. He did not say anything else so she phoned me. I asked her to hold the phone to Charlie's ear. She said she would, but added that Charlie would not be able to talk. I told her I understood, but I had something I needed to tell him.

I do not know how I knew what to say, but I retold him his story about being twins and knowing that he would become one soon. I reminded Charlie that each twin knew that becoming one was for the greater good and everyone would be fine. I used his words "we know" and stated he was going home. His wife came back on the line, said goodbye and hung up.

Charlie's wife called the next day to say that Charlie died very peacefully soon after our call.

CAITLYN

Caitlyn was 20 years old and a sophomore in college when she was diagnosed with a rare cancer. Her treatment took an extreme toll on her, and the cancer kept growing. One day I met with Caitlyn in the hospital. Her cancer was still growing rapidly, and they had only experimental treatment to offer. She was in great pain. Caitlyn wanted to go home and prepare to die.

I agreed to meet with one of her oncologists and advocate for her discharge. Not long thereafter, Caitlyn went home to her mother and father's house and prepared to die. This did not mean that she was happy or wanted to die, but that she had a conscious recognition of where she was in her life/death path.

I visited Caitlyn at home many times. As she prepared to die, she spoke of many things: her life and the people in it, the hopes and dreams she would never realize, and her fears. After much discussion, Caitlyn had two remaining fears to address: she had never known anyone who had died and feared that not knowing anyone would result in her being alone; and, ending her relationship with her mother. Caitlyn did not want to cause her mother any pain. She loved her mother very much and feared losing contact with her.

These fears were a topic of conversation each time we met. On one particular visit I asked Caitlyn if she had been going to the other side. Initially, she questioned what I was asking. I shared stories from others I had known who had spoken of and from the other side. I told her that many times dying people are visited by those from the other side who help them prepare for death. "Is that who she is?" Caitlyn asked. "Who?" I said. "The female, about my age, who comes to get me and shows me 'sneak previews' during my dreams." We then discussed these dreams and how Caitlyn could ask questions about her two fears when she is "over there."

Caitlyn did ask her questions, and the next time I saw her she was eager to tell me what she had learned. Caitlyn was meeting all kinds of people in many different places, which helped alleviate her fear of not knowing anyone, and assured her that she would not be alone. Many people would be waiting for her. When I asked Caitlyn about her mother she said, "We know this is for the greater good. My mother will be fine. She will be sad and she will understand." Caitlyn went on to explain how time is different there from what it is here. Everything happens at once there, and past, present and future are separate here in the physical world. Caitlyn understood and was comforted by knowing she would not really be missing her mother at all. Caitlyn was also calmed knowing "from the inside out" that the timing and circumstances of her physical death were "for the greater good."

Prior to her death, Caitlyn gave the name "angels" to those who visited her in her dreams, showing her sneak previews of the other side. Caitlyn had an angel poster above her bed at her mother's house. Caitlyn had always said 13 was a special number for her. Not long after resolving her fears and saying her goodbyes, Caitlyn died peacefully on the thirteenth. When she died, the angel poster above her bed fell to the floor.

DAVID

David was struggling with completing his school work and his responsibilities at home, so his mother suggested he come and talk with me. He was 23 years old and had returned to college, trying to finish this time. David was questioning the meaning of life, trying to find his purpose, and stated he felt he really needed to start over.

I asked David about his religious beliefs and what they had taught him about letting go and starting anew. David did not feel a close connection to the religious training he had received growing up. We explored many different forms of starting over - different religions, mythologies and spiritual traditions that shared the intent of stepping into a new life. I explained how in all traditions, ceremony is used to express transition, from what one used to be, to what one has become.

As David learned about the various traditions, the fire ceremony of indigenous cultures captured his attention. I explained how they would collect items to represent their past and present. Through the process of collecting, the ceremony would evolve. I gave David the homework to "collect" his life.

David came back to my office and brought all he had collected; three large yard bags stuffed with items representing all of his life. David described how he went through every drawer and closet in his bedroom. He sorted through every item, throwing out most things, but keeping those which best represented where he had been, and those things necessary to step into his new life.

David also went through the boxes filled with childhood memories which his mother had kept. He and his parents relived his grade school, middle school and high school years. They shared all their memories and stories, which they had not recalled or spoken of for years. David reported that as an only child his parents had focused very closely on everything he did and that going through the memory books allowed them to reconnect with their closeness and love of one another. They were able to let go of the worries of David's future and what he was going to do.

I asked David if he felt his collecting was complete and if he was ready to create his ceremony, consciously letting go of where he has been and stepping into the unknown, his next phase of life. David affirmed that he was ready. I guided David in creating his own sacred ceremony of transition, where he would create a fire and burn all he had collected. David eagerly left my office to complete his ceremony.

After his ceremony, David came to see me and said he felt excited and open to change. He knew his life was going to change in a big way, but he did not know how. On this visit, David also told me that he had gone to the doctor because he had a headache that would not go away.

David had gone to see his oncologist. When he was three years old David had a brain tumor. Through surgery and chemotherapy, he had been in remission for the past 20 years. Because of this history, his parents always kept a close watch on David, for no one knew if the cancer would come back.

Shortly after our session, David learned that his brain cancer had returned and that it was located in an inoperable location in his brain. He would die from this tumor.

When David shared this information with me he was calm. He spoke about the internal push he felt to go through everything to prepare for the fire ceremony. He knew it was the right time for him to die, that he now understood why he didn't finish college and couldn't figure out what to do with his life, because his life was ending. We discussed how he could help his parents, especially his mother, prepare for his impending death, as David was highly aware of the pain this was causing her.

The cancer grew quickly and took away David's physical abilities rapidly. I went to David's house where his mother was his primary caregiver. They had a hospital bed set up in the living room so David could look out the window and watch the birds. He especially liked the red cardinals and would point them out to his parents.

During one of my visits to their house, David told me privately that he knew he would be dying soon, and that he had started to go to the other side and come back. He described the other side as beautiful and warm, with wonderful music. He said he could now understand why things happen as they do. He was calm and accepting of his death. David also wanted to help his mother, father, family and best friend feel as calm as he did.

Not long after that visit, David went into a comatose state. His mother called me to say that one morning she came into the living room with the medicine tray, and David was looking at his hands. He turned to his mother and asked "Mom, am I alive or am I dead?" She dropped the medicine tray and ran to him. Crying, she said "You are alive." David was alert, could move all parts of his body, was hungry and speaking lucidly.

David told his mother that he wanted to see certain family members, his parents and his best friend. They all gathered and David spoke to them for two days. He told them how everything was just as it was supposed to be; he told them about forgiveness, what he had learned from them and how he loved them. He explained they would always be together and that they should not be sad for too long after he left. He explained that his death was for the greater good and that they would all soon understand, too.

David's mother explained to me that David seemed so well that she initially thought he had had a spontaneous remission and that the cancer was gone. But David kept saying that he would be leaving soon. He woke from the comatose state only to explain things and to help them understand. He wanted to thank his parents for all their love, and to let them know that they had done everything just right.

At the end of the second night, David told his parents it was time for him to leave. He asked his parents to leave the room and be together. David explained that he was going to die holding his best friend's hand. David's best friend agreed that he did not want to leave until David died.

David's parents went upstairs to their bedroom. David held his best friend's hand, said goodbye, and peacefully died.

NANCY

Nancy had metastatic breast cancer, and was thirty-nine years old when I met her. She was taking chemotherapy, had completed radiation treatment and was supplementing the medical protocol with herbs, vitamins and varying cleansing processes. She came to work with me when the cancer continued to progress even after several years of medical and complementary treatments.

Nancy began by asking questions regarding healing. We explored the many forms she had worked with and what others she was considering. I told Nancy of my belief that dying to the physical world is complete healing, so when I discuss healing, death is part of the continuum. That conversation led Nancy to investigate her beliefs about death.

Nancy and I had many conversations about what was important to her when she died. She recalled the deaths of people she knew and how she felt about their dying process. One experience had a great impact on Nancy. When her mother died very suddenly, no one was able to say goodbye. Nancy knew she wanted to say goodbye. Nancy also wanted to take care of all the business aspects of her life. She wanted to make sure that she did not leave a mess for anyone to clean up after she died. Once Nancy had addressed what was important to her when she died, she was able to focus her ever-dwindling amount of energy on healing and living.

There came a time when Nancy was in the hospital again, and the side effects from the chemotherapy were taking a toll on her physically. Nancy asked one of her family members to call me, requesting that I join them at the hospital. When I arrived, her father and siblings were all present. Nancy lay in the bed, very still, going in and out of a comatose state. Her family members informed me that several times when Nancy woke up she said she had seen their mother in the room, too. This was confusing to them and they wondered what was wrong with her. They wanted me to talk with Nancy.

I approached Nancy and leaned over her, quietly saying hello. Nancy opened her eyes, said "hi," and told me she had been waiting for me. She had things she wanted to say. At this time, Nancy was speaking very softly and even though her family members were near the end of her bed, they could not hear her clearly. So as Nancy spoke, I repeated her words loudly enough so all her family members could hear what she was saying.

Nancy took turns speaking individually to each family member. She recalled events from the past with each person. She told them she was sorry for certain things and asked their forgiveness of her. Nancy spoke of times that each person had hurt her, and she said she forgave them. Nancy spoke of what she cherished in her relationship with each of them and what she would miss in the future with them. Nancy also spoke about their futures and what they would be encountering. She gave them encouragement, support and suggestions for difficult circumstances in the times to come.

After Nancy spoke to them individually, she addressed them all saying it was her time to die. Their mother was there waiting for her to say her goodbyes. She told them she had no regrets. She understood the timing of her death and it was right. Nothing was missed (medically), there were no mistakes, and no one should be angry about her dying. Nancy told them all she loved them very much and would look forward to seeing them soon.

When Nancy finished talking, she closed her eyes and everyone left the room. I thanked Nancy for sharing part of her life with me and was the last to leave the hospital room.

Once I was out of the room, one of Nancy's brothers came up to me and began challenging me saying, "How did you know all those things? Why did you say those things?" Nancy's brother was very upset. I explained to him that I did not make up those things, but that Nancy had said them to me. I had merely repeated Nancy's words louder so everyone could hear, since Nancy was so weak and her voice was so soft. Her brother challenged me again saying "We could hear her and she was not talking in any language that I have ever heard before. Nancy was mumbling and making very strange sounds. You were saying those things and how did you know them?"

I was shocked, because I heard Nancy say everything that I repeated. I did not know any of the events Nancy was referring to, much less the details she described. I most definitely did not know about their futures and their children's futures. I explained again that I was repeating what I heard Nancy say. I did not know any of the details she described and could not repeat them at that moment. He did not believe me. I said I did not understand either but offered to meet with the brother and any of the family members at another time if that would be helpful to them.

I left the hospital confused and wondering what had just occurred. I had heard Nancy say all of those things and was just repeating them. In addition to Nancy's brother, all the other family members said they heard Nancy talking, but that it did not sound like any language they had ever heard, and they knew Nancy did not speak another language.

After Nancy died I spoke with several family members, including the brother who was so angry at me. They told me Nancy never regained consciousness and died peacefully several hours after we had all met with her. They were still perplexed by what I had said, but they found comfort in her words repeated by me. They also told me that several things Nancy had predicted for their futures had come true. It was those events which helped them to accept that Nancy had spoken to them, and I was just the conduit.

MICHAEL

"He has been to the other side again and now understands what is happening. That is why he is calm." I was returning Susan's call regarding her husband, Michael. He had just had his second seizure. Michael's first seizure scared him and lead to his diagnosis of brain cancer.

Michael was an exceptional man. Professionally, he was a brilliant Ph.D. physicist. Michael worked for a company where he invented many things which continue to be used today. In his personal life, he was deeply loving in his role as a compassionate husband, father and human being to all he knew. Susan herself was a remarkable woman. She was trained to respond to medical crises while a member of an emergency response medical team. After her husband's diagnosis, she became his primary caregiver. She understood all too well what his diagnosis meant.

As the cancer progressed, Michael was able to tell the doctors where the cancer was growing before the scans provided confirmation. He was also able to recognize what brain functions he was losing, and in what part of the brain they were located.

My phone call with Susan occurred not long after we first met. Through our time together we discussed conscious living and conscious dying and how that greatly differs from what we might want or like. Susan did not like her husband's rapid decline, but she was able to be with him each step of the way, providing the love, comfort and care necessary to support Michael's healing path. We discussed how being conscious of dying doesn't mean there is happiness about the human timing. The timing of any individual death is beyond our human ability to understand.

As the cancer progressed, I went to Susan and Michael's house to be with both of them. By this time, Michael was blind in his right eye and had lost most functions on the right side of his body. When Susan and I were together, many times I would make drawings with multiple colors to explain what I was saying. I spoke of these drawings with Michael and Susan as we discussed conscious dying as complete healing. Michael smiled broadly. He conveyed his agreement and understanding. We discussed how many people in their dying process are able to speak from "both sides." Michael smiled again and spoke about the research and inventions at his workplace, saying, "We know that there is so much more." While Susan and I pondered why this would be Michael's time to die and asked other questions unanswerable to us, Michael simply stated, "We can't tell you because you are not ready." I asked Michael if "We" meant he was speaking from the other side. Michael stated, "Yes, We are." It was clear that Michael understood why he was dying at that time, and that he accepted the timing. Although Michael was not able to share how he understood this, he had a calmness he was able to share with those he loved, especially Susan. He was able to speak to her about her future life without him, encouraging her to continue living and loving.

Michael was able to say all his goodbyes and express his love before he died. As his final moment came, Michael looked at Susan with love in his eyes and died with a smile.

MARIA

I met 27 year-old Maria when she first came to me with her husband. They explained that Maria had been dealing with cancer for the past year. She had gone through many types of treatment including a bone marrow transplant. She had had two recurrences since the transplant. They were no longer looking for a cure but were concerned with length of and quality of life. They were both afraid to discuss death, which is why they came to see me.

We discussed the three levels of healing: past, present and future. Maria referred to fear as her "denial room." Neither Maria nor her husband wanted to be in this place, i.e., discussing and preparing for Maria's death. They weren't even 30 yet! We discussed acceptance and facing death consciously as a process, not a linear set of steps. Maria openly stated she was angry with God.

They were heading on vacation, going back to where Maria grew up, and where they had met and fallen in love. We had discussed the importance of closure - saying goodbye knowingly to the places important to Maria that she would not see again. This was difficult to accept, yet Maria and her husband knew it was the reality of their current circumstance. At each location visited they made physical offerings. With the offerings they created a ceremony to acknowledge their experiences and memories from each location. They tearfully said goodbye to those times and places, knowing they would never be the same again. Maria would not be back physically, and when her husband visited again, it would be after Maria's death.

How to handle losses was a recurrent theme in our discussions. Maria had a list of losses to address: never having children, losing her ability to play as a concert flutist, not being able to run - the list went on. I explained my concept of coming even with life and death. For Maria, this meant not being happy about where she was but recognizing that this was her reality.

From that evenness, she would then walk toward her death with her eyes and heart wide open. This created a state of being aware of where they were each moment of each day. They knew what they could still do and could say good bye consciously to what they no longer could do together. The argument is about timing of life and death. Maria knew she was dying, and she could feel and see her body changing. We discussed that we, as humans, are not in charge of the timing of life and death. Our challenge is to be present where we are on that continuum so we can be present for each moment we are alive. The challenge is also recognizing and accepting that we have as many moments in a lifetime as we need, from a soul perspective.

Coming even with life and death brought Maria to accepting her impending death. She then stopped all medical treatment- chemotherapy, etc., since it was taking more of her life energy than what she received back. Maria and I discussed how she could leave her "soul print" when she died. This is much like a fingerprint, but it moves from her soul to another soul, and for those still living, it becomes a conscious memory to come back to when thinking about Maria after she dies. We discussed how the way she leaves the physical world is her last act of conscious teaching. Since Maria was so young, she had many friends and family watching how she left this world. Maria understood her role for others and with great courage, honor, and dignity spoke to all of her family and friends about her dying, saying goodbye consciously to each and every one.

The last time I met with Maria was a few days before she died. We met in her home with her husband. Maria and her husband did a beautiful job of discussing the final death preparations, including the specific recording of Maria playing the flute for her funeral. They spoke honestly of their love for each other, their shared days and their separate futures. Maria told her husband he needed to continue to live after she died. She encouraged him to get married again and raise a family. Maria thanked her husband for all the love and support he gave to her, helping her prepare for her final healing and death. Maria said she was ready to die and knew it was time. Maria no longer needed to say she was angry about the timing. She had an internal knowing that her death at that time was right.

Several days later, as Maria was in her husband's arms, she opened her eyes, said she loved him and died peacefully.

THOMAS

Thomas had bone cancer. I met him after many rounds of chemotherapy, when he was preparing for surgery on his spine. Again. His hope was that the surgeons would be able to remove the cancer and he could return to his life. He had a happy life, a good job, a wonderful wife and a four-year old daughter.

When we first met, I explained to Thomas that preparing for death in his own personal way would provide him with the opportunity to focus all his energy on healing, from the cancer and the impending surgery. Thomas did not immediately warm to this concept, but the more we discussed it, the more it made sense to him. Thomas realized that he was expending a great deal of energy worrying about what would happen to his wife and daughter if he should die. Together we addressed each of his desires and fears, should he die during his cancer treatment or surgery.

Once Thomas had neutralized his thoughts of dying, he focused on preparing for surgery. He worked with the image of all the healthy cells in his body surrounding and lifting out the cancer cells through the surgery. When he entered surgery, he was prepared for either outcome - life or physical death – and he was clear that his choice was to continue living.

One of the risks of surgery was that Thomas might never walk again. Thomas and his wife had spoken of how they would adapt the house if that should happen. Thomas did not talk with his wife about the possibility of his death. They just could not approach the subject. Thomas did not want to cause his wife any more stress than she already had from her multiple roles: taking care of him and their daughter, shouldering the household responsibilities and working full time. He knew how hard she was working and felt that preparing for his death was his personal work.

Following Thomas's surgery he was discharged to a physical rehabilitation center to recover from his back surgery and begin physical therapy. His wife called me to ask if I could meet her and Thomas once he had been transported. I agreed and left so that I would arrive shortly after he arrived. As I was driving to the physical rehabilitation center, I was overcome with the feeling that Thomas was actively dying at that time. I walked into the physical rehabilitation center and asked for directions to Thomas's room. The person at the desk asked me to wait. I was quickly met by a social worker who informed me that Thomas should not have been transported there. The physical rehabilitation staff thought Thomas might be dying, but were not certain since their therapeutic focus was on helping people return to their homes. They informed me that Thomas's wife did not understand how serious Thomas's condition was. As I entered Thomas's room, I met his wife and parents. Thomas's parents had driven in from out state to provide support to them during the surgery.

Thomas was going in and out of a comatose state. He was completely paralyzed from the neck down. When he was awake he was able to communicate and move his eyes. He asked his wife and parents where he was and who all the people in the room were. They did not know how to respond, since they did not see the people to whom Thomas was referring, some of whom were dead. Thomas's wife and parents were afraid of what was happening to Thomas.

When I leaned over Thomas, he opened his eyes, smiled, and said "Brenda, you are here." He asked me where he was - was he in his body or had he died? This scared his father who left, saying he would be taking care of his grand-daughter. I told Thomas there were many people who would describe this experience as "going between worlds." He smiled and agreed with that description. He asked me where he was going. I responded, "home." Upon hearing the word "home," Thomas's eyes rolled up, he stopped communicating and seemed to lose consciousness. In a brief period of time, Thomas opened his eyes again and said "Yes, home." Thomas was calm and stated he was going home, where he had been before.

I then asked Thomas about the people he needed to say goodbye to before he left here, the physical world, to go home. I asked about his daughter, and Thomas replied, "No, I said goodbye to her last night." He had already said goodbye to his father. He needed to say goodbye to his mother and his wife before he went home. Both of these women were in the room listening to our conversation. They were crying and in shock. His wife asked how he could be dying when he was at a rehab center. Thomas calmly replied, "We know this is for the greater good. You and our daughter will be fine. This is the right time for me to leave and go home."

Whenever Thomas was awake he answered his wife's questions, as she was trying to grasp her future changing from having a husband who couldn't walk to being a widow. Thomas also explained to his mother that the timing of his death was for the greater good. His mother

said goodbye and left to be with Thomas's
father and daughter.

Thomas continued to go in and out of a comatose state, between worlds. When Thomas's
awareness was not in the physical world, his
wife and I spoke of many of the concepts which
Thomas and I had explored together; conscious
living and conscious dying and how I believe
that when we completely heal, we die to this
world. She was becoming calmer. As her calmness grew she would ask Thomas different
questions when he woke, questions about her
future and her daughter's. Thomas would
respond to each question with "We know...."
All his responses were affirming that his wife
and daughter would be sad, but that they would
also be fine in their future together.

When Thomas was not conscious, his wife
called a friend to be with her until Thomas died.
I stayed with her until her friend came. Once
her friend arrived, Thomas's wife explained to
her that Thomas was dying. They would be together when Thomas died. I left them sitting
together next to Thomas.

Thomas's wife called me not long after I left and explained that Thomas died very peacefully that evening. He went home. Thomas's wife explained she appreciated having the opportunity to speak with Thomas during his dying process, and hear him calmly and joyfully describe where he was going. And while her grief was not lessened by this or by hearing Thomas explain "We know that this is for the greater good," his words helped her continue living, knowing that he died when he was supposed to and that he went to a place he called "home."

BARBARA

Barbara was 33 years old, and was a wife and a mother to two young children, one son and one daughter, when we met. She was receiving treatment for the recurrence of her cancer. In walking the balance between conscious living and conscious dying, she had come to terms with her past and where she was in her life. She made a conscious plan for dying and focused her energy on living and healing.

There was a point when Barbara knew she was on her personal fork in the road. As she looked to her death, she spoke to me of her concerns. With great courage, she addressed them one by one: planning her funeral, giving support to her husband who would be raising the children without her, preparing to say goodbye to her children, deciding what she wanted loved ones to have of her belongings, etc. One fear we discussed on multiple occasions was her fear of leaving alone and walking to the other side by herself. I told her that on the soul level I could walk with her to the other side up to the "black line." Once we reached the line, she would be with others and I would return. She would not be alone.

Barbara and I had many soul-based conversations. We both knew she was approaching her physical death but could not predict when in linear time it would be. At that time, I needed to leave the country to complete the process of adopting my Guatemalan child. I did not know how long I would be gone. Barbara and I discussed that I might not be in Minnesota when she was passing. She was concerned again about "going alone." I explained that on the soul level I did not need to be with her in the physical world to walk her over, reminding her to come find me, and we would walk together to the line. I left for Guatemala after saying my goodbyes.

One night while in Guatemala, I had a vivid dream that felt intensely real. Barbara came to me in the dream. We did not talk with our mouths or use words, but we understood each other, a knowing between the two of us.

The Dream

Barbara flew to me and asked me to come with her. She had on a long blue dress and a matching hat. Both had delicate bead work on them. She was holding lit candles in her arms. I followed her as she flew to many people. I was floating next to Barbara as she approached people and handed them a candle. We would then fly to the next person, to whom she handed a candle. I watched her hand out candles to many people I did not recognize, and to many of the family members I had met over the time Barbara and I had known each other. Her last candles, except one, went to her husband and two children. As she handed the candles to them, there was a feeling of love, warmth and understanding.

Barbara had one candle left when she looked at me and we flew up to the other side. As we approached, others came to greet her. Many were with her by the time Barbara and I arrived at the line. There she looked at me and handed me her final candle. Through our eyes we exchanged a depth of love and understanding. She turned and walked into the arms of those across the line. I returned to my physical body.

I woke up wondering where I was and what time it was. I turned to the clock and thought about the date. I had a strong sense that this was more than a dream.

When I returned home weeks later with my baby son, I picked up my work messages. There was a message from Barbara's husband asking me to call him. I did so, and after our initial greeting I said, "Before you tell me anything, may I give you a date and a time of a dream I had?" After giving him this information he asked, "How did you know when she died?" I told him about my dream. He explained that the clothing I saw her in was the beaded dress and hat she had chosen to be buried in. He explained how peacefully she died, and that those with her felt her presence as she left.

RACHEL

Rachel wasn't able to come into my office due to the many side effects she had from the chemo, so she called me instead. She was consciously walking to her physical death.

Rachel began telling me about a dream she had the previous night. It felt real to her and was very vivid. She had told her husband about the dream. She wanted to find out if I thought she was "crazy," like her husband did.

In the dream, Rachel's perspective was that of observing herself. Rachel went on to further describe her dream:

There was a house on top of a hill. Everything from "our world" was there. She was in a room in the house. In the dream, she watched as she found a "new door" in the house, one she had never seen before.

Rachel opened the door and found that all of the house on the hill and all that we know in "our world" were within a room on the bottom floor of a houseboat going down a river. As Rachel left this room (from the house on the hill) she saw a set of stairs leading to the upper deck of the houseboat. Rachel went up the stairs.

Once on the deck, Rachel felt, saw, smelt, heard and tasted how beautiful everything was. She had never felt such beauty and wondered why she hadn't noticed it before. She found she could merge with almost everything; she could merge and feel the deer on the side of the river as the houseboat went past. She could merge with the eagle soaring above her. She could feel the grass on the banks and the wind through the trees. She could merge with the entire houseboat, even the bottom gliding through the river. But she could not merge with the river.

The beauty was so amazing that Rachel went back down the stairs and through the door leading into the house on the hill where all that we know exists. Rachel went to find her husband to show him the door and where it leads. He would not come. She went to find other friends and family to show *them. But no one would come with her; they could not see the door. She went back out the door and up the stairs to the deck.*

Walking along the deck, Rachel went to the front of the boat and found many deck chairs where people could sit and watch the beauty flow by. Rachel said no one was there except me, Brenda. She sat down next to me and we had a conversation. We discussed the incredible beauty, how she had not noticed it before, how she could merge with everything but the water. She was confused why no one, including her husband, could see the door and come with her, except for me. In her dream, Rachel observed me explain to her that it wasn't their time yet, that we all see the door in our own time.

Rachel and I walked to and down the stairs and through the door that brought us back into the house on the hill, which contained the entire world that we know. As we walked, Rachel asked why she couldn't merge with the river. I explained to her that it hadn't been her time but it would be soon. I said she would merge with the river and return to all the waters. We then entered the house on the hill knowing we couldn't share what we knew.

After relating her dream, Rachel questioned why others couldn't follow her into the houseboat, and what the river could mean. Her husband didn't understand the dream and was confused in "real" life, too. I suggested the dream seemed to represent Rachel on her own personal houseboat flowing down the river of life, and that merging with the water represented her physical death and her soul reconnecting to all the waters.

This comforted her and she said it felt "right." Her last concern regarded her husband. She wanted me to explain the dream to him because she feared he thought she was crazy. I promised I would explain the dream to him. Later that day, Rachel peacefully merged with her river.

AFTERWORD

Please take what is helpful to you from these stories and leave the rest. May these stories be healing to you and your loved ones.

Blessings to you.

Brenda

ABOUT THE AUTHOR

Brenda Hartman, MSW, LICSW was working on two Ph.Ds when her life was interrupted by a diagnosis of stage 4 ovarian cancer. The life threatening diagnosis changed her life course from academics and research to becoming a therapist specializing in oncology. Facing death at a young age was an isolating experience. She made the commitment that if she lived, she would provide support and guidance to other cancer patients and their loved ones.

Brenda has been in private clinical practice since 1991. She has created and presented programs locally and nationally on the socio-emotional aspects of the cancer experience. As a 20+ year cancer survivor, she intimately understands the fear of dying. She volunteers for MOCA (Minnesota Ovarian Cancer Alliance) and is a patient representative for the Mayo Clinic SPORE (Specialized Program of Research Excellence) grant for ovarian cancer. She is a board member for the Alumni Board for The College of Education and Human Development at the University of Minnesota.

Brenda lives with her family in St. Paul Minnesota.

Made in the USA
Monee, IL
05 January 2024

51097121R00036